Author: Mary Moore

Proofreaders: Alison Hennell, Kieran Maguire.

Content Review: Alison Hennell, Kieran Maguire.

Editor: Kieran Maguire

Published by Adkins & Matchett (UK) Limited – trading as Adkins, Matchett & Toy

Second edition 2007

Manufactured in United Kingdom

ISBN: 978-1-891112-71-3

To order call: +44 (0) 1295 256 161 or +1 914 944 0999
Visit us at or buy online: www.amttraining.com

UK
Linden House, 55 South Bar
Banbury
Oxfordshire
OX16 9AB UK

T   +44 (0) 1295 256 161
F   +44 (0) 1295 272 108
E   info@amttraining.com
W www.amttraining.com

USA
235 Eastern Avenue
Ossining
New York
10562 USA

T   +1 914 944 0999
F   +1 914 944 0465
E   info@amttraining.com
W www.amttraining.com

AdkinsMatchett&Toy

Table of Contents

Introduction

THE BUSINESS CYCLE

Accounting should simply reflect what has actually happened to the business over the relevant time frame. Therefore, the first area to examine is the business cycle:

WHAT HAPPENS FIRST?

The shareholders invest money in the business and this is used to buy some assets with which to operate.

THE NEXT STEP:

These assets are used to trade profitably (hopefully!).

AND THEN:

This profit turns into cash. A vital step, since investors invest to make cash not rather than profit.

FINALLY:

This cash is either given back to the investors (in the form of dividends) or it is reinvested in the business.

THE TRICK:

Managing this cycle is key to running a successful business. There are several potential pitfalls. The rate at which cash is spent on assets may be faster than the rate at which those assets produce profits and hence cash. This puts enormous pressure on a new business and in recent years this has been referred to as "cash burn". If the cycle is working well, it will turn at a good rate, pay a reasonable cash dividend to investors and grow the business by reinvesting the remaining profits.

MANAGING THE BUSINESS EFFECTIVELY:

In order to manage the business effectively, we need to measure how many assets there are, how much profit is being generated, when the cash is coming in and how it is being spent. Accounting is little more than this process.

The asset piece is measured by the *Balance Sheet*, the profit and cash pieces are measured by the *Income Statement/Profit and Loss Account* and the *Cash Flow Statement* respectively.

> ### Accounting! What's it all about?
>
> Accounting should simply reflect what has happened in the business over the relevant time

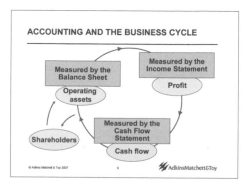

Let's examine each of these three key statements in turn.

THE INCOME STATEMENT/PROFIT AND LOSS ACCOUNT

The income statement/profit and loss account measures the sales made and costs incurred over a particular time period. For external reporting this is usually for a year but internally most businesses will prepare their income statement/profit and loss account on a weekly or a monthly basis.

The income statement/profit and loss account captures a sale when the product or service is delivered to the customer. Cash may or may not change hands at this stage.

Costs are recorded in the income statement/profit and loss account to reflect the costs of making the sales during that period. This is called the *matching* or *accrual* concept. This concept states that the costs recorded must match to the sales made in the relevant time period.

FOR EXAMPLE:

If a business sold 20 product items in a week, the income statement/profit and loss account for that week should include the purchase cost of those 20 items along with the rental cost of the warehouse and the staff costs for that week.

Although the jargon in an income statement/profit and loss account may vary (especially from country to country) the costs are always deducted from sales in order of how closely they relate to the sale itself. The order of cost deduction is therefore:

1. Cost of products sold
2. Sales, general and administration costs
3. Interest expense
4. Tax expense

> **Matching! What's it all about?**
>
> In the income statement/profit and loss account sales are matched with costs for the relevant time period.

This is illustrated in the following diagram:

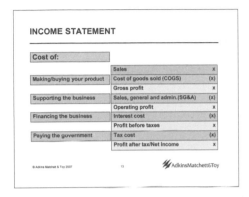

SO LET'S BUILD AN INCOME STATEMENT:

Ryan Inc – Income statement for the month of May!

Scenario:

During May, Ryan Inc sold 120 products at a price of $100 each. 20% of these customers paid in cash. Ryan Inc is a reseller, and these products cost $45 each. The monthly cost of two employees (one responsible for sales and one for administration) is $3,000. Ryan Inc's quarterly rental cost of the office space they use is $3,000. Ryan Inc do not need warehouse space since they deliver direct from their supplier to the customer. The average monthly cost of utilities is $560. Ryan Inc has a bank loan of $10,000 incurring a monthly interest rate of 0.5%. The tax rate is 30% of profits.

Solution:

Sales (120 * $100) = $12,000. Whether they have been paid in cash or not is irrelevant for the purposes of building the income statement/profit and loss account.

Cost of goods sold (120 * $45) = $5,400. Again, whether the supplier has been paid or not is irrelevant for the purposes of building the income statement.

SG&A (3,000 + 1,000 + 560) = $4,560. The rental expense has been divided by 3. This reflects one months' cost rather than the cost of the whole quarter.

Interest expense (10,000 * 0.5%) = $50

Tax expense (Profit before tax * 30%) (see below)

Sales	12,000
Cost of goods sold	5,400
Gross profit	6,600
SG&A	4,560
Operating profit	2,040
Interest expense	50
Profit before tax	1,990
Income tax (1,990*30%)	597
Net income/profit after tax	1,393

SO WHAT HAPPENS TO PROFIT?

The bottom line profit (net income/profit after tax) belongs to the shareholders and consequently is reflected as part of shareholders' equity on the balance sheet. More will be covered on this in the balance sheet section below.

The income statement/profit and loss account will be covered in more detail in the next chapter.

THE BALANCE SHEET

The balance sheet shows the position that the business is in at the **end** of the relevant period. It shows the assets the business controls, its liabilities and the amount of equity belonging to the shareholders. The reason it is called the balance sheet is because total assets must equal liabilities and shareholders' equity as illustrated below:

The Balance Sheet! What's it all about?

Assets = Liabilities and Equity

The Fundamental Accounting Equation

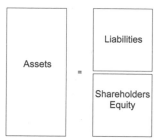

The two sides must always equal or *balance!*

The liabilities and equity section shows where the business gets its funds and the assets section shows how those funds have been used.

The assets section is divided into two sub-sections, showing short-term and long-term assets. In this context, a long-term item is one whose life in the business is expected to be longer than one year.

Examples of long-term or fixed assets are:

- Property
- Plant and machinery
- Financial investments that are to be held for the long-term
- Patents
- Licenses

Short-term assets are those whose lives are shorter than one year and include:

- Inventories/stocks
- Accounts receivables/debtors (when credit is given to customers)
- Prepayments
- Cash
- Financial investments that are to be held for the short-term only

Liabilities are also broken down into short and long-term items. Short term liabilities include:

- Accounts payable/creditors (when credit is taken from suppliers)
- Income taxes payable
- Short-term borrowings (where the repayment date is within one year)

Long-term liabilities include borrowings where the repayment date is longer than one year from the balance sheet date. More detail on all these areas will be covered in the working capital, and debt and equity chapters.

Shareholders' equity consists of two elements. Capital represents shares bought by investors when the business was set up. This represents the cash that was physically given to the business by the shareholders. The second (and very often more significant) piece is retained earnings/profit and loss reserve. This is the cumulative profit earned that has not been paid to the owners in dividends but has been reinvested in the future growth of the business instead.

Neal Inc – Shareholders' equity and retained earnings!

Neal Inc has been trading for the last four years. The investors initially invested $12,000 into the business in return for shares. Since then net income has been as follows:

Year 1	(3,000)
Year 2	1,500
Year 3	4,200
Year 4	4,500
Total	7,200

Dividends were not paid for the first two years. In years 3 and 4 dividends of $1,000 were paid each year.

In the balance sheet at the end of year 4 shareholders' equity will show the following:

Capital invested	12,000
Retained earnings (7200-2000)	5,200
Shareholders' equity	17,200

The $12,000 was actively invested in cash, whereas $5,200 (-3,000 +1,500+4,200+4,500–1,000–1,000) retained earnings were invested "passively" by not taking all the profits out via dividends.

THE CASH FLOW STATEMENT

This shows how cash has been generated and used over the relevant period.

Most cash flow statement styles will present the flows of cash using three main categories:

- Operating cash flows
- Investing cash flows
- Financing cash flows

> **Back to Basics!**
>
> *Sales is vanity*
> *Profit is sanity*
> *Cash is reality*

Operating cash flows include the flows from the core operations of the business and is driven by trading.

Investing cash flows deal with any investments in the future of the business. Any new plant and equipment would be included in this section.

The financing section deals with any investments made by shareholders and any dividends paid to them. Any new borrowings or any repayments of existing loans would also be shown in this section.

SO HOW DOES IT ALL WORK THEN?

THE BALANCE SHEET MUST ALWAYS BALANCE

For each transaction the effect of the balance sheet must be considered and duly recorded. Joe set up a business last year. Let's follow him into the second year of trading:

Joe Inc

The balance sheet at the end of his first year of trade was as follows:

Cash	1,500
Inventories/stocks of chilli lights	300
Fixed assets	1,100
Total assets	**2,900**
Payables/creditors	300
Debt	1,500
Common Stock/Ordinary Shares	1,000
Retained earnings	100
Total Liabilities & Equity	**2,900**

Joe wants to expand and has persuaded his family to buy shares. He issues new shares for $2,000.

Assets	=	**Liabilities and Equity**
Cash ↑ $2,000		Equity ↑ $2,000

Joe buys a consignment of pink fluffy poodles for cash. They cost $400.

Assets	=	Liabilities and Equity

Cash ↓ $400

Inventory ↑ $400

Joe repays $1,000 to the bank.

Assets	=	Liabilities and Equity

Cash ↓ $1,000   Loans ↓ $1,000

Joe buys some office furniture for $500.

Assets	=	Liabilities and Equity

Cash ↓ $500

Fixed assets ↑ $500

Joe pays $100 to the chilli light supplier.

Assets	=	Liabilities and Equity

Cash ↓ $100   Payables ↓ $100

Joe sells the fluffy toys for $1,100 cash. A profit of $700 is therefore made.

Assets	=	Liabilities and Equity

Cash ↑ $1,100   Equity ↑ $700

Inventory ↓ $400

Joe pays himself a $500 salary paid in cash.

Assets	=	Liabilities and Equity

Cash ↓ $500   Equity ↓ $500

WHAT DOES THE BALANCE SHEET LOOK LIKE NOW?

Don't forget Joe's opening balances from last year. You can check last year's balance sheet for Joe's business on the slides.

Cash (see below)	2,100
Inventories/stocks (300 + 400 − 400)	300
Fixed assets (1,100 + 500)	1,600
Total assets	**4,000**
Payables/creditors (300 − 100)	200
Debt (1,500 − 1,000)	500
Common Stock/Ordinary Shares (1,000 + 2,000)	3,000
Retained earnings (see below)	300
Total Liabilities & Equity	**4,000**

AND WHAT ABOUT THE INCOME STATEMENT/PROFIT AND LOSS ACCOUNT?

Sales	1,100
Cost of goods sold	400
Gross profit	700
SG&A	500
Net income/profit after tax	**200**

AND HOW DOES THIS FIT INTO THE BALANCE SHEET?

Beginning retained earnings	100
Net income for the period	200
Ending retained earnings	300

It is the ending retained earnings number that sits in the balance sheet.

AND WHAT ABOUT THE CASH FLOW STATEMENT?

Cash from sales	1,100
Cash paid to suppliers	(500)
Cash paid to employees	(500)
Operating cash flow	100
Equipment purchased	(500)
Investing cash flow	(500)
Share issue	2,000
Debt repaid	(1,000)
Financing cash flow	1,000
Net cash flow	**600**

Important!

Dividends are paid out of cumulative (retained) earnings not just the profit for that period!

AND HOW DOES THIS FIT INTO THE BALANCE SHEET?

Beginning cash	1,500
Net cash flow	600
Ending cash	**2,100**

It is the ending cash number that appears in the balance sheet.

AND WHAT ABOUT "DEBITS" AND "CREDITS"?

What you must be able to do is understand how transactions are recorded as shown above. Debits and credits are simply the language used by accountants to describe how to record a transaction. Like all languages it is based upon a set of rules that should be diligently applied so that everyone using the language can understand each other. The rules for using debits and credits are as follows:

Asset ↑	Debit
Asset ↓	Credit
Liabilities & Equity ↑	Credit
Liabilities & Equity ↓	Debit

Each transaction can have a different number of debits and credits depending upon the nature and complexity but:

TOTAL DEBITS MUST ALWAYS EQUAL THE TOTAL CREDITS!

So for some of Joe Inc's transactions above:

Joe wants to expand and has persuaded his family to buy shares. He issues new shares for $2,000.

Assets	=	**Liabilities and Equity**
Cash ↑ $2,000		Equity ↑ $2,000

Debit Cash	$2,000
Credit Equity	$2,000

Joe buys a consignment of pink fluffy poodles. They cost $400 and he paid in cash.

Assets	=	**Liabilities and Equity**
Cash ↓ $400		
Inventory ↑ $400		

Debit Inventory	$400
Credit Cash	$400

Joe repaid $1,000 to the bank.

Assets	=	**Liabilities and Equity**
Cash ↓ $1,000		Loans ↓ $1,000

Credit Cash	$1,000
Debit Loan	$1,000

Joe sells the fluffy toys for $1,100 cash.

Assets	=	Liabilities and Equity
Cash ↑ $1,100		Equity ↑ $700
Inventory ↓ $400		

Debit Cash	$1,100
Credit Inventory	$400
Credit Equity	$700

Joe pays himself a $500 salary paid in cash.

Assets	=	Liabilities and Equity
Cash ↓ $500		Equity ↓ $500

Debit Equity	$500
Credit Cash	$500

The Income Statement/Profit and Loss Account

REVENUES AND COSTS

There are four areas that we must consider when reviewing the income statement/profit and loss account. How are sales or revenues recorded? How are costs or expenses dealt with?. How do the key accounting links work? What are the main measures of performance?

WHEN REVENUES ARE INCLUDED:

When a business records revenues or sales we must understand exactly what this means. Does it mean that the contract has been signed? Or does it mean that the product or service has been delivered and the cash received? Understanding this line item is fundamental to understanding business performance.

The income statement or profit and loss account!

Remember?

It shows the sales/revenues less costs/expenses for a given time period.

WHEN AND WHERE COSTS ARE INCLUDED:

It is also crucial that we understand what is meant by a cost or expense item. Firstly we must appreciate when the costs show up in the income statement/profit and loss account. Secondly we must understand where costs appear on the income statement/profit and loss account.

Since there are many line items for costs in the income statement/profit and loss account, in order to understand the nature of the business's performance we must know where business costs are presented.

KEY ACCOUNTING LINKS:

It is crucial to have a strong understanding of the engineering of accounting. Knowing the fundamental links between the accounting statements will enable you to do two things.

Firstly, it will help analyze the information you are presented with by the corporation.

Secondly, it will help you predict the impact on financial performance of specific transactions (a key area if you work in an advisory or sales role).

KEY INDICATORS OF PROFITABILITY:

And last but by no means least we need to understand the main performance indicators used to measure profitability.

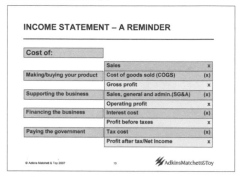

INCOME STATEMENT – A REMINDER

Cost of:		
	Sales	x
Making/buying your product	Cost of goods sold (COGS)	(x)
	Gross profit	x
Supporting the business	Sales, general and admin.(SG&A)	(x)
	Operating profit	x
Financing the business	Interest cost	(x)
	Profit before taxes	x
Paying the government	Tax cost	(x)
	Profit after tax/Net Income	x

© Adkins Matchett & Toy 2007   13   AdkinsMatchett&Toy

SALES/REVENUES

Sales are recognized in the income statement/profit and loss account as ***the product/service is delivered***. This means that the income statement/profit and loss account is designed to reflect the work actually undertaken by the business. It is not designed to show when the sales were "won" or when the cash is actually received.

FOR EXAMPLE:

If a business sold and delivered 20 product items in a week, then the income statement/profit and loss account for that week should include the sale price of those 20 items in its sales/revenue line. If however, it simply signed a contract to deliver those 20 product items in 2 months time then nothing would be recorded in the income statement/profit and loss account for that week.

Imagine the business received payment in advance, so that it signed the contract and received the monies. The income statement/profit and loss account still would not show the sale of those 20 items since they have not yet been delivered.

WHY IS THIS ALL SO IMPORTANT?

Because growth in sales is often a key indicator of an investment opportunity. Sales are also a fundamental driver of profitability. However, the quality of those revenues is paramount. By quality, we mean the speed with which they turn in to cash.

AND WHERE DOES CASH COME IN?

There are three possibilities:

1. customers could pay on delivery as with a retailer;
2. they could be given credit. This only really happens when the customer is another business; or
3. they could prepay.

> **Sales/Revenues and the income statement/profit and loss account!!**
>
> **Sales are recognized in the income statement/profit and loss account as the work is done not as the money is received.**

SO LET'S TAKE EACH IN TURN:

Padley Inc – is a retailer

As a retailer, Padley Inc receives cash from customers as the product is "delivered".

Assets	=	Liabilities and Equity
Cash ↑		Retained earnings ↑ (sales ↑)

The sale value is recorded in the sales line on the income statement/profit and loss account as the product is delivered. This will automatically increase retained earnings (part of shareholders' equity, on the balance sheet). At the same time the cost price will be transferred from inventories to COGS. This will also flow through to retained earnings and the net effect is that the profit on the sale is captured in retained earnings.

Russell Inc – is a manufacturing business

As a manufacturer, Russell Inc gives credit to customers. This means that the cash is received sometime after the product is delivered.

Assets	=	Liabilities and Equity
Receivables/debtors ↑		Retained earnings ↑ (sales ↑)

When the product is delivered, sales/revenue is recorded in the income statement/profit and loss account.

When the cash is received, the cash increases and the receivables decrease. There is no income statement/profit and loss account impact at this stage.

Pound Inc – is an airline

Airlines usually get paid in advance of delivering the service. This means that they "owe" a flight to their customer. This is recorded as a liability, often called "deferred revenue".

Assets	=	Liabilities and Equity
Cash ↑		Deferred revenue ↑

When the customer takes the flight then sales are recognized since the airline has now "delivered" the service.

Assets	=	Liabilities and Equity
		Deferred revenue ↓ Retained earnings ↑ (sales ↑)

> **Accruals/Matching**
>
> **Costs or expenses feed into the income statement/profit and loss account to** match with sales or the time period

COSTS/EXPENSES

Costs or expenses in the income statement/profit and loss account are recognized when the "benefit" is consumed or "used up". Most cost items are "used up" by the selling process but some are used up as time passes.

For example, the benefit of having an item of inventory/stock is consumed as soon as the item is sold. On the other hand, the benefit of having office space is consumed over time as you occupy the space. This process of matching sales with the costs of achieving those sales or with the time period within which they were made is called *matching or accrual*.

SO LET'S LOOK AT SOME SPECIFIC EXAMPLES:

We are going to run through the most common practical applications of this conceptual process. We will apply this to inventories, prepaid items and long-term assets.

INVENTORIES/STOCKS:

When inventory/stock is first purchased it is recorded in the inventory/stock asset on the balance sheet. This recognizes that it is an asset since it will provide benefit to the business sometime in the future. As soon as it is sold, this benefit has been "used up" which means it should be recorded as a cost in the income statement/profit and loss account. This is done in cost of goods sold (COGS).

This can be illustrated as follows:

Graham Inc – buys some inventory for cash

Assets	=	**Liabilities and Equity**
Inventory/stock ↑		
Cash ↓		

The income statement/profit and loss account is unaffected since no trading has taken place. Any benefit from the inventory/stock has not yet been used up so no cost is recognized. This only happens when the product is sold. When the product is sold, the benefit of having inventory/stock is used up and a cost is therefore recognized in the income statement/profit and loss account.

Assets	=	**Liabilities and Equity**
Inventory/stock ↓		Retained earnings ↓
		(COGS ↑)

Inventory/stock and retained earnings decrease in recognition of the sale of product having an associated cost.

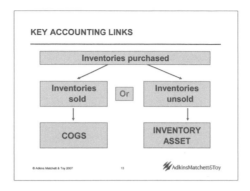

PREPAID ITEMS:

With some cost items it is common for the item being purchased to cover a time period rather than for a specific delivery of a product or service. Examples of this are property rental or an insurance contract. It is also common practice for these items to be paid in advance for an agreed time period. This poses a problem when building the income statement/profit and loss account since although the item has been paid for, it has not been consumed or "used up". The solution is very similar to that which was adopted for the prepaid airline ticket, which we discussed under the sales/revenues section above.

The prepaid item (or prepayment) is allocated to assets in the balance sheet initially reflecting the fact that a "future benefit" is available from that item. In this case, the relevant asset is *Prepaid items or prepayment..*

As the insurance or rental is used up over time an appropriate proportion is transferred from the asset into costs/expenses in the income statement/profit and loss account.

This can be summarized as follows:

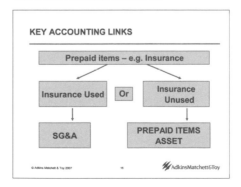

And the accounting works as follows:

Pally Inc – pays for rental for the next quarter

On 1 January Pally Inc pays for property rental for the following quarter.

Assets	=	**Liabilities and Equity**
Prepaid assets ↑		
Cash ↓		

The income statement/profit and loss account is unaffected since no rental has been used up. Any benefit from this cost will only be used as time passes. At the end of January one third of the rental has been used up and so one third of the cost should be transferred from the prepaid asset to the income statement/profit and loss account.

Assets	=	**Liabilities and Equity**
Prepaid assets ↓		Retained earnings ↓
		(SG&A ↑)

The prepaid asset decreases and retained earnings go down in recognition of the benefit of that cost being used up over the month.

USING UP LONG TERM/FIXED ASSETS – DEPRECIATION/AMORTIZATION:

Exactly the same thing happens whether the assets are short-term like insurance or property rentals or long-term like machinery. Also, often the time frame over which they will be used is not definite. Some manufacturing equipment is a typical example. The engineers responsible for maintenance may say that the life of the asset will depend on how many hours it is used or on how many items it produces. This is a complex issue and, in reality, this is a subject with many variables to consider. Nevertheless, for the purposes of building our income statement/profit and loss account we must make some assumptions about how the asset will be used up. In simple terms, we estimate the expected life of the asset and then we allocate the relevant proportion into the income statement/profit and loss account over that lifetime. This cost is called *depreciation.*

For example:

Judith Inc – buys a machine

Judith Inc buys a machine, which is expected to have a five year life.

Assets	=	**Liabilities and Equity**
Fixed assets ↑		
Cash ↓		

The income statement/profit and loss account is unaffected since no benefit of having the machine has yet been gained and no cost has been used up. The fixed assets or property, plant and equipment (PP&E) in the balance sheet reflects the future benefit that will be gained from this machine. Any benefit from this cost will only be used as the machine is used for production. At the end of the first year one fifth of the machine has been used up and this proportion of the cost should be transferred to the income statement/profit and loss account.

Assets	=	Liabilities and Equity
Fixed assets ↓		Retained earnings ↓ (COGS or SG&A↑)

The fixed asset decreases and retained earnings go down in recognition of the benefit of that cost being used up over the year.

TAX EXPENSE

The tax expense number is calculated by taking the profits before tax and multiplying by the relevant tax rate. This is an *accrued* tax number and therefore does not give information about when these taxes must be paid in cash. It simply tells us what the tax expense is based on the profits reported. If those profits are also reported in the current period's tax return then it is due for payment in accordance with the payment rules of the relevant jurisdiction.

There can be items which are not reported on the current period's tax return. In this case this element of the tax expense is referred to as deferred taxes. The footnotes usually provide a breakdown of the tax expense into the current and deferred tax elements.

BUT WHERE DO THESE COSTS APPEAR?

When doing any analysis, it is helpful to know where these costs will appear in the income statement/profit and loss account. Whilst there is often only one category for sales/revenues, in all income statements/profit and loss accounts the costs are broken down into several subcategories. Most income statements/profit and loss accounts will have the following cost categories:

Cost Categories!

COGS – production
SG&A - support

- Cost of goods sold or Cost of sales (COGS)
- Sales, general and administration (SG&A)
- Interest income or expense
- Tax expense

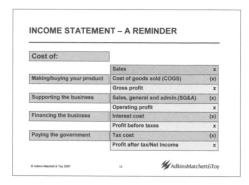

COGS or SG&A?

COGS (or cost of sales) are production related, whereas SG&A covers the cost of supporting the trading of the business. SG&A is where marketing and accounting function costs would be included. Some cost categories will be included under both headings. For example, depreciation for production equipment will be included in COGS whereas depreciation of non-production equipment will be in SG&A.

WHAT ABOUT NON-RECURRING OR UNUSUAL COSTS?

These are problem items especially when you are doing trend analysis on the business performance. They cause volatility in the numbers and can distort your analysis. For this reason, they should be identified or highlighted.

They are often called **extraordinary or exceptional items** and may appear in several places in the income statement/profit and loss account:

- Embedded in an existing line item (COGS or SG&A)
- As a separate line item above the tax expense line
- As a separate line item but below the tax expense line

For example, any line item such as "Other income or expenses" should always be investigated to see if it contains a non-recurring item. Integration costs, following an acquisition, are a classic example of a non-recurring item. Many businesses categorize their restructuring costs as "non-recurring" also but when they frequently engage in such programs, you, the analyst, may disagree with such categorization.

KEY INDICATORS OF PROFITABILITY

There are several levels of profitability shown in the income statement/profit and loss account and it really depends on your viewpoint whether they are suitable for the analysis you are undertaking. In summary, the income statement/profit and loss account shows the following:

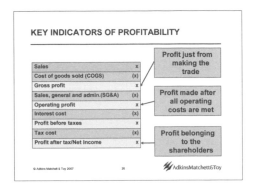

EBIT

EBIT stands for *earnings before interest and taxes*. It is designed to be a measure that indicates how well the business is performing just from doing what it is in business to do. It is very close (and indeed often identical to *operating* profit). However, many people using this measure are doing so in order to form a view about the future EBIT and consequently do not want it distorted by any non-recurring items. In practice, it is frequently adjusted to remove the effect of any such items. *This is a judgment call but normally EBIT will be "cleaned" for non-recurring items.*

It is easiest to think of EBIT as being the earnings from the parts of the business which are:

- **C**ore
- **C**ontinuing and
- **C**ontrolled

Jackson Inc

Jackson has the following income statement/profit and loss account. Calculate EBIT.

Sales	4,100
COGS	2,255
Gross Profit	1,845
SG&A	1,025
Operating profit	820
Integration costs	300
Restructuring expenses	175
Interest expense	48
Profit before tax	297
Tax expense	107
Profit after tax	190
Discontinued businesses	42
Net income	148

In this case, according to the strict definition of EBIT, the answer is $345 (297 + 48 or 820 – 300 – 175). The problem with this is that any view of the future EBIT potential of the business is likely to be understated. The integration costs or the restructuring expenses are

unlikely (unless you have evidence to the contrary) to be part of the income statement/profit and loss account next year. In this case most practitioners will "clean" the numbers and will treat the *ongoing EBIT* as $820 (345+300+175). This is before interest, taxes and non-recurring items.

EBITDA AND EBITA

EBITA stands for *earnings before interest, taxes and amortization*. It only removes amortization . In principle, amortization is the same as depreciation but it applies to intangible assets. The single biggest and most common intangible asset is goodwill, which arises as a result of an acquisition of another business. Most people would agree that this is not a normal operational item and consequently EBITA will measure the earnings from normal operations. Since goodwill is no longer amortized in most countries EBITA is less commonly used than in the days when income statements/profit and loss accounts had large goodwill amortization expense numbers.

EBITDA stands for *earnings before interest, taxes, depreciation and amortization*. It is a particularly common earnings measure in the world of banking and there are two main reasons for this. The first is that it approximates to *cash income*. Depreciation and amortization never result in a cash flow. (This happens when the asset is first purchased). EBITDA removes these non-cash items.

The second reason for using EBITDA is because it removes differences (between companies) relating to depreciation and amortization. EBITDA is very useful when working across international boundaries since accounting methodologies for depreciation and amortization can vary significantly.

Jackson Inc

Using the income statement/profit and loss account above for Jackson Inc, calculate EBITA and EBITDA assuming that there is depreciation of $145 embedded in the operating costs and amortization of $90 embedded in SG&A.

Using clean EBIT as the starting point, EBITA is $910 (820 + 90) and EBITDA is $1,055 (820 + 90 + 145).

NET INCOME

Net income is the profit generated on behalf of the shareholders after taking account of the obligations to the providers of debt capital. If you wish to form a view of the future net income number then this too must be "cleaned" for non-recurring items. *Normalized* net income is *after* all costs but *before* non-recurring items.

Net income is an after tax number so when adjusting for non-recurring items you must be careful to adjust for the after tax non-recurring amount. Frequently you are only provided with pre-tax information so therefore you need to estimate the post-tax number by taking the pre-tax information and multiplying by (1–the tax rate).

Jackson Inc

Using the income statement/profit and loss account above for Jackson Inc, calculate normalized net income assuming a tax rate of 35%.

Reported net income is $148 but this is distorted by two non-recurring amounts, the restructuring expense of $175 and the discontinued business expense of $42. These non-recurring items are materially different from each other and this can be identified by where they appear in the income statement/profit and loss account. The restructuring expense of $175 is shown before the tax expense line and therefore it is assumed to be pre-tax. The estimated post-tax equivalent is $114 (175 * 35%). The discontinued business expense is shown below the tax expense line, however, so therefore it can be assumed that this is a post-tax number already.

Therefore normalized net income is $304 (148 + 114 + 42).

Working Capital

There are four areas that we must consider when reviewing working capital.

- What it is?
- Why it is important?
- How the key accounting links work?
- What are the main performance measures?

WHAT IS WORKING CAPITAL?

Working capital is defined as *Current assets less current liabilities.* This is the investment in the assets and liabilities of the business that have a very short life. For example, an accounts receivable asset or debtor may only exist for days or a taxes payable liability may exist for months. This contrasts with long-term or fixed assets that may exist for many years or long-term debt that may have a life of years.

CURRENT ASSETS:

Current assets are expected to have a life of less than one year and come in a variety of types but the most common are:

- Cash
- Short-term investments
- Prepaid items/prepayments
- Accounts receivable/debtors
- Inventories/stocks

> **Working Capital**
>
> **Current assets**
> **Less**
> **Current liabilities**

Cash needs no explanation but the management of this item is one to be carefully considered for any successful business. Having lots of cash is ineffective since it will probably attract a very low rate of interest. The best thing to do is to invest in the business itself by buying new assets. However, this may not be possible at a given time, so surplus cash is often invested for the short term in short maturity investments. These investments allow fast access to your money but give a better return than leaving it on deposit.

Prepaid items arise when you pay for services in advance of using them. Insurance and property rental are examples. The prepaid asset decreases as the service is used up.

Accounts receivables/debtors arise when you sell on credit to your customers. Instead of giving you cash they promise to pay you in an agreed number of days.

Inventory/stock represents the product sitting in the warehouse waiting to be sold. As more products are made or purchased this asset increases and as products are sold, it decreases.

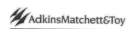

CURRENT LIABILITIES:

Current liabilities are liabilities whose life is expected to be less than one year and commonly include the following:

- Overdraft/credit facility
- Short-term debt
- Accounts payable/creditors
- Accrued expenses/accruals
- Taxes payable

An overdraft or credit facility is agreed with the bankers in advance. It works by allowing the business to "go into the red" or have a negative cash balance up to an agreed amount. This liability shows the amount of this facility used at the balance sheet date.

Short-term debt is a loan that is due for repayment within one year.

Accounts payable/creditors and accrued expenses/accruals are almost the same thing but they have a very practical difference. Accounts payable/creditors arise when you take credit from your suppliers. Accrued expenses/accruals also represent the amounts owed to suppliers. The difference between them is whether or not the business has received the invoice before the date of the balance sheet. For example, a product is delivered to the warehouse on the last day of the accounting year and is accepted by the warehouse staff. The invoice is likely to take some time to reach the accounting department. In the meantime, the accounting staff estimate the relevant amount and put it into accrued expenses/accruals. When the invoice is received it will be transferred to accounts payable/creditors.

Taxes payable represents amounts owed to the government for taxes due.

WHAT IS OPERATING WORKING CAPITAL/NET WORKING INVESTMENT?

Operating working capital, sometimes called net working investment is the same as working capital, but only includes those current assets and current liabilities that are driven by the trading operations of the business. Cash, short-term investments, overdraft/credit facilities and short-term debt are all driven by decisions made about cash management (which is not operational) and are therefore not included in the operating working capital calculation. Accounts receivable/debtors, Inventories/stocks and accounts payable/creditors are all examples of accounts driven by the day-to-day activities in which the business engages, which are operational.

Operating Working Capital

Operating current assets
Less
Operating current liabilities

As a general rule:

Operating working capital	=	Current assets – cash	–	Current liabilities – debt

Spectrum Inc – Working capital and operating working capital

The following is an extract form the balance sheet of Spectrum Inc.

Cash and cash equivalents	2,020
Marketable securities	48
Receivables/debtors	3,064
Inventories/stocks	1,480
Prepaid items/prepayments	300
Current assets	**6,912**
Accounts payable/creditors	3,398
Short-term borrowings	371
Dividends payable	136
Income taxes payable	129
Current liabilities	**4,034**

Working capital is $2,878 (6,912 – 4,034). In order to calculate **operating working capital** we must first consider which items are not driven by the day-to-day operations of the business. This can be a tricky decision but is helped by experience.

Cash and cash equivalents and marketable securities are not normally considered to be part of the day to day operations of the business. Decisions about how they are managed are normally organized by the treasury function within the business and are more to do with overall financing strategy than with trading operations.

Accounts receivable/debtors and Inventories/stocks are part of the day-to-day operating activities of the business.

Prepaid items are generally part of day-today operating activities. The most common items in this category are items such as property rental and insurance, which are certainly part of the core business operations.

Short-term borrowings are financing activities rather than operating. What about dividends and taxes? Taxes are driven by profits and the day to day trading of the business drives profits. Therefore taxes are normally an operating item. Consequently taxes payable are part of operating working capital. On the other hand, dividends have nothing to do with day to day operations. They are a return to the owners of the business and decisions regarding this item are made at the highest levels of the business.

In this case OWC (operating working capital) is 1,317 (3,064+1,480 +300–3,398–129).

WHY IS THIS IMPORTANT?

Current assets use cash and current liabilities supply cash. Some current liabilities are interest bearing (such as short-term debt), so this cash supply has an interest cost associated with it. However, suppliers don't normally charge interest when the business takes credit. This therefore represents "free financing".

Consequently, it seems logical that current assets should be kept as small as possible, where as current liabilities (particularly operating ones) should be kept as large as possible.

The problem here is that the business may be skating on thin ice and if some suppliers demand payment then the current assets may not be sufficient to meet this demand. In a worse case scenario, this is what causes business to "go bust" or bankrupt.

Even if it is not as bad as this, it can still cause serious problems. For example, you may lose sales by not having enough inventories/stocks to guarantee required delivery times. Alternatively your supplier, unhappy at all the free credit you are taking, may refuse to deliver any further product to you and this means that the factory line is "down" for several days while you sort out the mess!

If you are analyzing the performance of a business, then it stands to reason that you must gain a firm understanding about how good the business is at walking the *working capital tightrope.*

KEY ACCOUNTING LINKS

We are going to run through the most common components of working capital, examine their key accounting links and cover some of the practical issues affecting each item in turn.

INVENTORIES/STOCKS:

Remember our example from the chapter on the income statement/profit and loss account:

Graham Inc – buys some inventory/stock for cash

Graham Inc buys some inventory/stock for cash

Assets	=	**Liabilities and Equity**
Inventory/stock ↑		
Cash ↓		

The income statement/profit and loss account is unaffected since no trading has taken place. Any benefit from the inventory/stock has not yet been used up, so therefore no cost is yet recognized. This only happens when the product is sold. At this stage, the benefit of having inventory/stock is used up and so a cost is recognized in the income statement/profit and loss account.

Assets	=	**Liabilities and Equity**
Inventory/stock ↓		Retained earnings ↓
		(COGS ↑)

Inventory/stock decreases and retained earnings go down in recognition of the product sale having an associated cost.

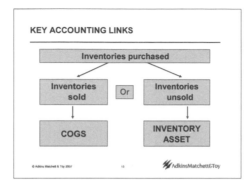

We can summarize this very quickly and easily using a **BASE analysis.**

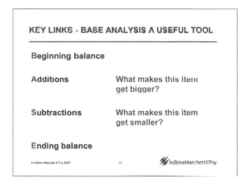

But how does this work for inventories/stocks? Well they go up as we buy or make a new product and they go down as we sell the product. So this is what it looks like for inventories/stocks.

INVENTORY/STOCK ISSUES:

This assumes that we know the cost of our products. Yet this is unlikely because prices change. So if the cost price changes, how do we know which price to transfer to COGS and which to leave in inventory/stock?

Corporations have policies to deal with practical issues such as these and in this case two of the possible policies are FIFO and LIFO.

FIFO - First in first out

LIFO - Last in first out

FIFO is more common because it matches with good physical management of inventory/stock, but a significant minority of businesses use LIFO so you do need to be aware of it and its implications.

Butterworth Inc – buys some stock

Butterworth Inc buys two items of inventory/stock: the first for $100 and the second for $120. During the period, one of these items is sold (and consequently its cost should be transferred to COGS).

The total cost of both products is $220, regardless of which policy is used.

Using FIFO, COGS is $100 (because the first to be sold is the first one in). Inventory/stock is therefore reduced by $100 to $120.

Using LIFO, COGS is $120 (because the first to be sold is the last one in). Inventory/stock is therefore reduced by $120 to $100.

The method chosen will affect reported profits, as the COGS figure used in both methods is different. We can draw some conclusions from this example:

In times of rising prices, LIFO gives lower profits and lower inventory/stock. And visa versa for FIFO.

Kim Inc – buys some inventory/stock

Kim Inc started in business on 1 January and has the following transactions in the month:.

Jan 1	purchased	100 items	@ $10 each
Jan 12	purchased	80 items	@ $11 each
Jan 20	purchased	120 items	@ $12 each
Jan 4	sold	95 items	@ $25 each
Jan 15	sold	86 items	@ $26 each
Jan 21	sold	112 items	@ $27 each

First, add up the total items bought and sold. In this case, 300 items were purchased and 293 were sold. This means that there are 7

FIFO!
How to calculate COGS!

First in First out!

LIFO!
How to calculate COGS!

Last in First out!

Items In Inventory/stock at the end of January. The question is how we allocate the cost of the items sold.

The next step is to calculate COGS.

The last thing is to calculate inventory/stock by comparing total cost with the COGS number from the previous step.

If we use FIFO:

COGS = (100*10) + (80*11) + (113*12) = 3,236

Total cost of products = (100*10) + (80*11) + (120*12) = 3,320

Inventory/stock = (3,320 – 3,236) = 84, or (7*12) = 84

If we use LIFO:

COGS = (120*12) + (80*11) + (93*10) = 3,250

Total cost of products = (100*10) + (80*11) + (120*12) = 3,320

Inventory/stock = (3,320 – 3,250) = 70, or (7*10) = 70

Note: Under LIFO the profit will be lower (because COGS is higher) and the inventory/stock is also lower. LIFO is not allowed in some countries because it normally produces lower profits. The tax authorities don't like it as they would receive less tax from corporations.

On a practical point, most corporations do this calculation at the end of a period and ignore the detail of the dates in and out. This makes the calculation easier and is called the *periodic inventory method.*

ACCOUNTS RECEIVABLE/DEBTORS AND BAD DEBTS:

We know that accounts receivable/debtors are monies owed to us by customers. But what if the customer is likely to default? This is a judgment area, but accounting normally takes a *conservative or prudent view.*

If we anticipate that a customer will not pay then we should "write off" the receivable/debtor. We reduce the amount showing as receivables/debtors. Retained earnings also reduce and this item appear as an income statement expense, within SG&A. It is part of the cost of giving credit to customers.

PREPAID ITEMS/PREPAYMENTS:

Remember the example of a prepaid item covered in the previous chapter?

Pally Inc – pays for rental for the next quarter

Pally Inc buys pays for property rental for the following quarter

Assets	=	Liabilities and Equity
Prepaid assets ↑		
Cash ↓		

The income statement/profit and loss account is unaffected since no rental has been used up. Any benefit from this cost will only be used as time passes by. At the end of the first month, one third of the rental has been used up and one third of the cost should be transferred to the income statement/profit and loss account.

Assets	=	Liabilities and Equity
Prepaid assets ☐		Retained earnings ↓ (SG&A ↑)

The prepaid asset decreases and retained earnings go down in recognition of the benefit of the cost being used up over the month.

ACCOUNTS PAYABLE/CREDITORS:

The accounting for accounts payable/creditors is straightforward. They represent the liability to pay our suppliers in situations where we have taken credit from them.

ACCRUALS OR ACCRUED EXPENSES:

As discussed above accrued expenses is a "holding account" for accounts payable/creditors and is where items are put after we have bought the product/service but before we have received the invoice.

KEY PERFORMANCE INDICATORS:

The most common ratios used to measure working capital are *days* ratios. These are commonly calculated for inventories/stocks, receivables/debtors and payables/creditors.

OPERATING RATIOS

$$\text{Receivable days} = \frac{\text{Average receivables}}{\text{Sales}} \times 365$$

$$\text{Payable days} = \frac{\text{Average payables}}{\text{Cost of goods sold}} \times 365$$

$$\text{Inventory days} = \frac{\text{Average inventories}}{\text{Cost of goods sold}} \times 365$$

© Adkins Matchett & Toy 2007   26   AdkinsMatchett&Toy

BUT WHAT DO THEY MEAN?

Inventory/stock days tell you how many days, on average, products are in the warehouse. It is measured from the time the item is received into the warehouse until the date it is delivered to the customer.

Payable/creditor days tell you how many days, on average, it takes to pay suppliers. It is measured from the time the item is received from the supplier until the date they are paid.

Receivable/debtor days tell you how many days, on average, it takes to receive monies from customers. This is measured from the date the product is delivered to the customer until they pay.

Note: Inventory/stock and payable/creditor days measure from the day product comes IN but receivable/debtor days measure from the day product goes OUT.

Alex Inc – Days ratios!

Alex Inc has inventory/stock days of 21, payable/creditor days of 30 and receivable/debtor days of 20.

This means that they actually receive cash from customers, on average, on day 41 (for 21 days the product sits in inventory/stock. It is then delivered to the customer who takes 20 further days to pay).

In terms of cash flow, Alex Inc needs to find funding for a cash cycle gap of 11 days (day 41 for cash in but day 30 for cash out).

Understanding the working capital cycle and its impact on cash is crucial but it varies significantly from sector to sector. You always need to ensure that you are comparing like with like.

Here are two businesses that have very different operating characteristics:

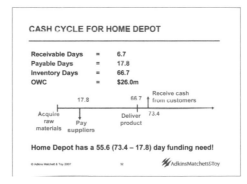

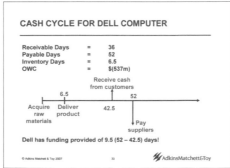

Fixed/Non-Current Assets

There are four areas that we must consider when reviewing fixed/non-current assets. We need to understand:

- what they are;
- why they are important;
- how the key accounting links work; and
- what the main measures of performance are.

WHAT ARE FIXED/NON-CURRENT ASSETS?

Fixed assets are those assets which are expected to provide benefit for the business for *more than one year*. They can be broken down into three main types:

- Tangible assets
- Intangible assets
- Financial investments

> **Fixed/Non-Current Assets**
>
> **Those which will be held for more than one year!**

TANGIBLE ASSETS:

Tangible assets are the most common type of fixed/non-current assets often called PP&E (property, plant and equipment). They have physical form and generally include items such as:

- Property
- Plant and equipment
- Fixtures and fittings
- Vehicles

INTANGIBLE ASSETS:

Intangible assets have no physical form and there are issues about whether they should be recognized as assets at all. As accounting only recognizes them as assets if they have been purchased, many businesses have significant levels of intangible assets which are not represented on the balance sheet. This is not because they do not exist but because they are home grown.

Examples of intangibles on balance sheets include:

- Goodwill
- Patents
- Licenses

Goodwill is the premium paid when another business is purchased. It is normally the largest component of intangible assets on balance sheets.

FINANCIAL INVESTMENTS:

Financial Investments represent investments in other businesses where the intention is to hold the investment for more than one year.

These types of investments may include equity affiliates (associates) or joint ventures, which occur when the business makes a strategic investment in another business. The business buys an equity stake, but is not simply an equity investor (who expects dividend returns

and possible capital growth). The owner normally is involved, to a greater or lesser degree, in the running of the business.

WHY ARE THEY IMPORTANT?

Fixed/non-current assets represent a significant and long-term investment and therefore such investment decisions need to be monitored carefully. Good decisions about fixed/non-current assets are often the difference between a successfully performing and a poorly performing business. Not only are they expensive but the consequences of mistakes can affect performance for many years.

KEY ACCOUNTING LINKS

Fixed/non-current assets are expected to provide benefit to the business over a number of years. Therefore they are shown on the balance sheet as a long term asset. However, over time this benefit will be used up and this needs to be reflected in the income statement/profit and loss account as a cost. This process is referred to as *depreciation* for tangibles and *amortization* for intangibles.

DEPRECIATION:

How do we calculate depreciation? First we need to estimate how long we are going to get benefit from the asset. Next we need to estimate how much the asset is going to cost overall. We already know the purchase price but we may very well recover some of this if we sell the asset when we are finished with it. This is called *salvage/residual value.*

Now we can calculate the amount we need to depreciate. This is the purchase price less any expected salvage value. We then divide this by the number of years over which we expect to benefit, to give the annual depreciation expense. This methodology is called *straight line depreciation* and is by far the most common method used by businesses.

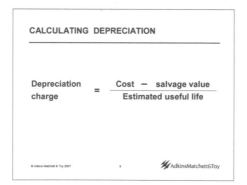

Some depreciation methodologies recognize that the charges should be higher in the earlier years rather than later years. There are various ways of calculating this. The most common is the reducing balance method. Here a % rate is applied to the purchase price less accumulated depreciation. This gives a reducing depreciation expense year on year.

Neville Inc

Neville Inc buys a machine for $142,200, paid in cash.

Assets	=	Liabilities and Equity
PP&E ↑		
Cash ↓		

When the asset is first purchased, cash decreases and property, plant and equipment will increase by the purchase price, in this case $142,200.

The life of the asset is estimated at 6 years and the salvage value is estimated at $12,000. This means that the depreciable amount is $130,200 (142,200–12,000) and the annual depreciation expense is $21,700 ($130,200/ 6).

Assets	=	Liabilities and Equity
PP&E ↓		Retained earnings ↓

PP&E and retained earnings decrease by the amount of the annual depreciation ($21,700) in recognition of the cost of the usage of the asset.

At the end of this first year the balance sheet will show the PP&E asset at $120,500(142,200 21,700). This is often called the *net book/carrying value* or *net book/carrying amount*. It is simply the purchase price of the asset net of accumulated depreciation.

Some balance sheets show the detail as follows:

Gross amount	142,200
Accumulated depreciation	21,700
Net book/carryin amount	120,500

Other balance sheets simply show the net amount on the face of the balance sheet and the detail can be found in the footnotes. In any event, it is the *net amount* of PP&E assets which is added into the balance sheet assets figure not the gross amount.

We can summarize this using a *BASE analysis.*

BASE ANALYSIS NET FIXED ASSETS

Beginning balance	Net PP&E
Additions	Capital Expenditure (new assets)
Subtractions	Depreciation
Ending balance	Net PP&E

© Adkins Matchett & Toy 2007   14   AdkinsMatchett&Toy

WHAT ABOUT ASSET SALES?

Let's continue with this same asset. Say this asset is sold at the end of the second year for $100,000 cash.

First calculate the net book value at the date of the sale.

Gross amount	142,200
Accumulated depreciation	43,400
Net book/carrying amount	98,800

We need to do two things to record the sale:

- The cash must increase by $100,000
- The assets must go down by $98,800

This means that the balance sheet will not balance, unless we record the difference between these two items. This is referred to as the gain or loss on sale. In this case it is a gain on sale. This can always be calculated as follows:

> **Gain or loss on sale**
>
> | | |
> |---|---|
> | *Selling price* | *X* |
> | *Net book amount* | *(X)* |
> | *Gain/(loss) on sale* | *X* |

Selling price	100,000
Net book amount	98,800
Gain on sale	1,200

Assets	=	**Liabilities and Equity**
PP&E ↓		Retained earnings ↑
Cash ↑		

Any gain is generally embedded as a negative number in the cost line where the depreciation on this asset was normally allocated. If it is a significant amount then it may be highlighted as a non-recurring item. However, for most businesses, asset disposals are not a significant economic issue.

Resistance Inc – Fixed assets and BASE analysis!

Resistance Inc has the following balances in the balance sheet at the beginning of the year:

Gross PP&E	447,800
Accumulated depreciation	198,300
Net book/carrying amount	249,500

During the year new assets were purchased at a cost of $280,700 and depreciation of $193,400 was charged. An asset with a net book amount of $88,600 was sold for $80,000. It had been purchased originally for $160,000.

Prepare a **BASE analysis** to reflect these changes. To do this when there has been an asset sale we have two choices:

First, we can analyze the net book amount (most commonly done) but extend it to deal with the asset sale. In this case it will look as follows:

BASE ANALYSIS NET FIXED ASSETS

Beginning balance	Net PP&E
Additions	Capital Expenditure
Subtractions	Depreciation
Subtractions	Assets sold (net amount)
Ending balance	Net PP&E

Applied to Resistance Inc will give us the following:

Beginning balance	249,500
Add – Cap. ex..	280,700
Subtract – Depreciation	(193,400)
Subtract – Asset sold (net amount)	(88,600)
Ending balance	248,200

Alternatively, we can analyze the gross and the accumulated depreciation numbers separately as illustrated below:

BASE ANALYSIS GROSS FIXED ASSETS

Beginning balance	Purchase price of all assets
Additions	Capital Expenditure
Subtractions	Assets sold (original purchase price)
Ending balance	Purchase price of all assets

© Adkins Matchett & Toy 2007   17   AdkinsMatchett&Toy

BASE ANALYSIS ACCUMULATED DEPRECIATION

Beginning balance	Acc. Depn. of all assets
Additions	Depreciation expense
Subtractions	Acc. Depn. of sold assets
Ending balance	Acc. Depn. of all assets

© Adkins Matchett & Toy 2007   18   AdkinsMatchett&Toy

Applied to Resistance Inc will give us the following:

Gross amount

Beginning balance	447,800
Add – Cap. ex.	280,700
Subtract – Asset sold (gross)	<u>160,000</u>
Ending balance	568,500

The accumulated depreciation on the sold asset is $71,400 (160,000 – 88,600), calculated by comparing the gross amount with the net book amount. Now we can analyze the accumulated depreciation.

Accumulated depreciation

Beginning balance	198,300
Add – Deprecation	193,400
Subtract – Asset sold (Acc. dep.)	71,400
Ending balance	320,300

And when we put these together we get the same answer as when we analyzed the net numbers.

Gross amount	568,500
Accumulated depreciation	320,300
Net book amount	248,200

KEY PERFORMANCE INDICATORS:

The following ratios are very useful when examining the fixed/non-current assets of a business:

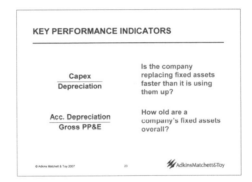

BUT WHAT DO THEY MEAN?

If there is no inflation and a business is replacing fixed assets exactly at the rate at which they are being used up then capital expenditure divided by depreciation will equal one. However, businesses do not operate in a non-inflationary environment so this ratio is likely to be larger than one, even when the assets are being replaced as they are being used up. This is because the new asset bought will be more expensive than the old asset being disposed of. Nevertheless, it gives a flavor of the efficiency of the asset base.

Comparing accumulated depreciation with gross PP&E gives you an indication of the age of the assets. You can then make an assessment of their efficiency and when they need to be replaced.

Debt and Equity

There are three areas that we must consider when reviewing debt and equity. We need to:

- understand the sources of funding for a business;
- the characteristics of both debt and equity; and
- how the key accounting links work.

THE SOURCES OF FUNDING

Businesses can source their funding by borrowing money or by obtaining investment from shareholders. Each of these routes has advantages and disadvantages.

> **Debt or Equity**
>
> **Debt holders have a FIXED claim on the business assets**

Lenders advance money which will be repaid to them over the course of time as agreed in the loan contract. They will only ever receive the original amount of the loan. This means that any increase in the value of the business is of no relevance to a lender. Their claim is for the amount of the principal only. Over time they will be paid interest at an agreed rate. In the event of the business being wound up the lenders will be repaid before the shareholders.

Shareholders are owners or "equity" investors. There is no contract to repay their initial investment. However, they can recoup this by selling their shares. Shareholders are paid dividends but the timing and the amount of these payments is not guaranteed. The shareholder receives their return in the form of dividends and by the potential increase in value of the business (and hence in the share price).

The most significant difference between debt and equity is *that debt has a fixed claim on the assets of the business whereas equity does not.* For example, if you buy a house with some of your own money and some borrowed money, any increase in the value of the house belongs to you, not to the lender. So If the value of the business increases over time, any debt amounts will stay fixed and the value of the equity will increase as illustrated below.

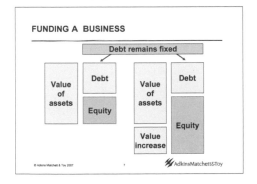

DEBT

Debt can be short-term (due for repayment within one year) or long-term (due for repayment anytime after a year). Long-term debt can be repaid in two ways:

- by a "bullet" repayment where the principal is repaid in one single repayment at the end of the loan; or
- by installments, in which case the principal decreases over the life of the loan in accordance with the repayment schedule.

PRESENTATION IN THE BALANCE SHEET:

Short-term debt will be shown under current liabilities and long-term debt under long-term liabilities. However, long-term debt will eventually become short-term debt when the repayment date is less than one year away.

For example if we borrow $100,000 to be repaid as a bullet at the end of 10 years, this debt item will appear in long-term liabilities for the first 9 years and then will be shown under current liabilities for the last year. If this debt is to be repaid in equal annual installments over 10 years then initially, $10,000 will be shown in current liabilities and $90,000 in long-term liabilities. At the end of the first year the amount owed reduces to $90,000 of which $10,000 is current and $80,000 is long term. This can be illustrated as follows:

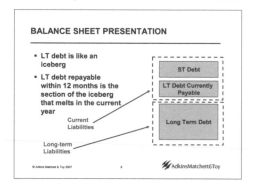

KEY ACCOUNTING LINKS:

Accounting for debt follows normal accounting principles. When the loan is taken out, both cash and debt increase. When repayments are made, cash and debt decrease. Interest is a cost and so retained earnings will decrease as interest is accounted for. This will show in the interest expense line of the income statement. Debt can be summarized using a **BASE** analysis as follows:

BASE ANALYSIS LOANS/DEBT

Beginning balance	Total debt
Additions	Interest incurred & new debt issued
Subtractions	Payments made (principal & interest)
Ending balance	Total debt

© Adkins Matchett & Toy 2007   15   AdkinsMatchett&Toy

EQUITY

There are two main types of equity:

- common stock or ordinary shares; and
- preferred stock or preference shares.

Both common stock/ordinary share and preferred stock/preference shareholders will receive dividends if they are declared by the board of directors. However, the amount of the preferred stock/preference share dividend is fixed and agreed up front. In the event of a "winding up" the preferred stock/preference shareholders get paid before the common stock/ordinary shareholders. As a result, preferred stock/preference shareholders are taking on less risk but do not share in the upside like the common stock/ordinary shareholders do.

Each share has a "par" or "nominal" value. The price at which the shares are issued (first sold by the business) is generally above par and the difference is know as the "premium" or "additional paid in capital".

Number of shares!

Watch this! Make sure you are using the correct number

The fixed dividend for preferred stock/preference shareholders mentioned above is always quoted as a % of par. Any dividend paid to the common stockholders/ordinary shareholders must be decided by the board of directors of the business.

The **Authorized** number of shares is the maximum number of shares that the business is legally allowed to issue. This can be changed if the shareholders wish.

The *Issued* number of shares is the number of shares that have been issued by the business. This will increase if there is a new share issue.

The *outstanding* number of shares is the number of shares currently owned outside the company. This will increase if there are new shares issued and will reduce if there are shares repurchased by the business.

PRESENTATION IN THE BALANCE SHEET:

The par value multiplied by the number of shares is shown as *share capital* or *common stock* on the balance sheet.

The difference between issue price and par value multiplied by the number of shares is shown as *share premium* or *additional paid in capital* on the balance sheet.

Shares repurchased are normally shown as a negative number in *treasury stock*, which is a negative item in shareholders' equity.

KEY ACCOUNTING LINKS:

When shares are issued, cash increases and shareholders' equity also increases. However, in the shareholders' equity section, the monies raised must be divided into par value and premium/additional paid in capital as discussed above.

Dividends are paid out of the pot of earnings called "retained earnings". When they are paid, retained earnings and cash decrease.

If the business repurchases shares, cash and shareholders' equity decreases, by purchase price multiplied by the number of shares purchased. As mentioned above this often is shown in a line item called **Treasury Stock** which is a negative component of shareholders' equity.

RETAINED EARNINGS:

Profit after tax or Net income belongs to both types of shareholders. An agreed fixed amount will be paid to the preferred stockholders/preference shareholders first, with the remainder belonging entirely to the common stockholders/ordinary shareholders. Some of this may be paid to them as a dividend with the rest being reinvested in the business.

The amount reinvested in the business is shown in shareholders' equity on the balance sheet and is normally called retained earnings (sometimes called the profit and loss account reserve).

Using *BASE* analysis is an effective way of analyzing the retained earnings number and it works as follows:

BASE ANALYSIS RETAINED EARNINGS

Beginning balance	Retained earnings
Additions	Net income
Subtractions	Dividend
Ending balance	Retained earnings

© Adkins Matchett & Toy 2007   24   AdkinsMatchett&Toy

© Adkins, Matchett & Toy 46 www.amttraining.com

Cash Flow Statement

WHAT IS A CASH FLOW STATEMENT?

In addition to preparing an income statement and balance sheet, a company must prepare a **cash flow statement**. A cash flow statement simply describes the flows of cash into and out of the business over one year. The cash flow statement is like your bank statement. It shows how cash came in and went out.

> **Cash flow statement**
>
> **A reconciliation of two balance sheets!**

HOW TO BUILD A CASH FLOW STATEMENT

The trick to building a cash flow statement is to *use the balance sheet* as the main information source. Mathematically, the cash flow statement is always a reconciliation of the effect on cash of the difference between the beginning and ending balance sheets.

FOUR RULES:

There are four golden rules of cash. They are:

FOUR RULES

1. **Assets rise** :	**cash falls**
2. **Assets fall** :	**cash rises**
3. **L&E rise** :	**cash rises**
4. **L&E fall** :	**cash falls**

© Adkins Matchett & Toy 2007   8   AdkinsMatchett&Toy

Let us go through each one in turn:

> **Four Rules!**
>
> *Assets up* – *Cash down*
> *Assets down* – *Cash up*
> *L&E up* – *Cash up*
> *L&E down* – *Cash down*

An example of an asset increasing is capital expenditure. This is highly likely to involve a cash outflow; therefore the effect on cash of *an asset increase* is a *cash decrease*.

An example of an asset decreasing is the payment by a customer of amounts owing. This involves a cash inflow; therefore the effect on cash of an *asset decrease* is a *cash increase*.

An example of liabilities and equity increasing is a new loan. This will involve a cash inflow; therefore the effect on cash of *a liability and equity increase* is a *cash increase*.

An example of liabilities and equity decreasing is the payment of a dividend. This will involve a cash outflow; therefore the effect on *cash of a liability and equity decrease* is a *cash decrease*.

Alison Inc – part 1

	Last year	This year	Change	Cash Flow
Cash	1,300	1,195	Answer	Answer
Inventories	300	325	25	(25)
Receivables	200	190	(10)	10
Net PP&E	1,100	1,250	150	(150)
Total assets	**2,900**	**2,960**		
Payables	300	330	30	30
Debt	1,500	1,375	(125)	(125)
Common stock	1,000	1,100	100	100
Retained earnings	100	155	55	55
Total L and E	**2,900**	**2,960**		

	Cash Flow this year
Inventories	(25)
Receivables	10
PP&E	(150)
Payables	30
Debt	(125)
Common stock	100
Retained earnings	55
Net cash flow	**(105)**

And how does this fit into the balance sheet?

Beginning cash	1,300
Net cash flow	(105)
Ending cash	**1,195**

It is the ending cash number that sits in the balance sheet.

ORGANISING THE CASH FLOWS

Cash flows are generally organized into three types:

- Operating cash flow
- Investing cash flows
- Financing cash flows

Operating cash flows are those which arise as a result of day to day operating activities, such ascash from customers, , paying bills to suppliers and paying salaries.

Investing cash flows are those which arise as a result of investments in the future growth of the business. Capital expenditure, investments in stocks and bonds are all examples of investing cash flows.

Financing cash flows includes any cash flows relating to financing the business through debt and equity. Paying dividends, repaying or issuing debt and issuing equity are all examples of financing cash flows.

Alison Inc – part 2

The purchase of fixed assets are investing cash flows. A business's objective for buying fixed assets will be to enhance profits! Therefore, buying fixed assets, otherwise known as capital expenditure, is an investing cash flow.

Inventories/stocks, receivables/debtors and payables/creditors are all operating cash flows (since these are core day to day activities in which the business engages).

Debt and common stock finance the business and give rise to financing cash flows.

What about retained earnings? Well, these increase as we make profits and profits are driven by the core operations of the business therefore this will be an operating cash flow.

The reorganized cash flow statement will look like this:

	Cash Flow
Net Income	55
Change in inventories	(25)
Change in receivables	10
Change in payables	30
Operating cash flows	**70**
PP&E	(150)
Investing cash flows	**(150)**
Decrease in debt	(125)
Increase in shares	100
Financing cash flows	**(25)**
Net cash flow	**(105)**

PRACTICAL PROBLEMS

It is often too simplistic to simply take the change between the beginning and ending balance sheet numbers and decide whether the cash arises as a result of operating, investing or financing activities. There are two areas where this is very likely to be inappropriate. Let's take each in turn and work through their impact using the example above.

RETAINED EARNINGS:

Alison Inc – part 3

So far, we have decided that the change between beginning and ending earnings is entirely due to net income. We calculated this to have been 55 (155 – 100). *But* what if you know, from the income statement, that net income was 85! This means that the numbers don't make sense unless some other item is affecting the retained earnings number. We know from our understanding of the key accounting links that retained earnings is also affected by dividends.

We can use our *BASE* analysis to help solve the conundrum;

 AdkinsMatchett&Toy

CASH FLOW STATEMENT

Beginning retained earnings	100
Net income	85
Dividends	???
Ending retained earnings	155

In order for these numbers to fit together the dividend must have been 30 (100 + 85 – 155).

This means that the change in retained earnings has two components:

- **net income** is driven by operations; and
- **dividends** is a financing item.

We can adjust our cash flow statement accordingly:

	Cash Flow
Net income	85
Change in inventories	(25)
Change in receivables	10
Change in payables	30
Operating cash flows	**100**
PP&E	(150)
Investing cash flows	**(150)**
Decrease in debt	(125)
Increase in shares	100
Dividends	(30)
Financing cash flows	**(55)**
Net cash flow	**(105)**

DEPRECIATION:

The other area that we have simplified is the PP&E analysis. In our example above, we have said the difference between the beginning and ending PP&E balance is due to capital expenditure of 150 (1,250-1,100).

However, what if the footnotes to the financial statements indicate that depreciation of 134 was expensed in the year. This highlights two problems:

- the first is that capital expenditure is not 150; and
- the second is that depreciation is not a cash flow.

Let's start by using a **BASE** analysis to understand the PP&E numbers:

Beginning PP&E balance	1,100
Capital expenditure	???
Depreciation	134
Ending PP&E balance	1,250

This means that capital expenditure must have been 284 (1,250+134–1,100).

However, if we put that amount into our cash flow statement it will no longer work because the net cash flow will not give the correct ending balance for cash in the balance sheet.

To solve this problem, let's remind ourselves about the key accounting links for depreciation:

Assets	=	**Liabilities and Equity**
PP&E ↓		Retained earnings ↓

Remember, retained earnings will decrease as COGS or SG&A increase as they will contain the depreciation charge. This will in turn cause net income to decrease, which feeds into retained earnings.

So if we "clean" the PP&E number for the depreciation effect, we must also "clean" the net income number since it is also affected.

Another way to look at this is to say that the net income has been reduced by a non-cash item and if we are using this as the starting point for building our cash flow we must "zero – out" the effect of any non cash items. Depreciation reduced net income, so to "zero – out" its effect we must add it back.

So the cash flow statement now looks like this:

	Cash Flow
Net income	85
Depreciation	134
Change in inventories	(25)
Change in receivables	10
Change in payables	30
Operating cash flows	**234**
PP&E	(284)
Investing cash flows	**(284)**
Decrease in debt	(125)
Increase in shares	100
Dividends	(30)
Financing cash flows	**(55)**
Net cash flow	**(105)**

THE STEPS:

Now let's work through a full example together:

Shirley Inc

Shirley Inc has the following income statement and balance sheets. You would like to see the cash flow statement but you need to build it from the information you have.

Income Statement

	Income Statement
Sales	1,785
COGS	982
Gross profit	803
SG&A	393
Operating profit	410
Interest expense	60
Profit before tax	350
Tax expense	116
Net income	**234**

Included in operating costs is a depreciation expense of 275.

Balance Sheet

	Last year	This year
Cash	1,019	1,000
Inventories	98	108
Receivables	188	156
Prepaid items	45	54
Net PP&E	803	892
Total assets	**2,153**	**2,210**
Payables	119	134
Taxes payable	88	96
Debt	1,100	904
Common stock	158	168
Retained earnings	688	908
Total L and E	**2,153**	**2,210**

STEP 1 – CATEGORIZE THE CASH FLOWS USING THE BALANCE SHEET:

Cash	*The answer*
Inventories	*Operating*
Receivables	*Operating*
Prepaid items	Likely to be items such as rental and insurance. Therefore Operating.
PP&E	Capex is *Investing* but depreciation should be in the *Operating* section
Payables	*Operating*
Taxes payable	*Operating*
Debt	*Financing*
Common stock	*Financing*
Retained earnings	Net income is *Operating* but the dividend is *Financing*

STEP 2 – BUILD ANY SUPPLEMENTARY CALCULATIONS NECESSARY:

You should consider a *BASE* analysis for PP&E and Retained earnings. Also, many bankers put all the operating working capital items together rather than including each item into the cash flow in its own right. If this is the case it is useful to calculate the beginning and ending OWC first.

PP&E BASE

Beginning balance	803	
Capital expenditure (plug)	364	(892 +275 – 803)
Depreciation expense	275	
Ending balance	892	

Retained earnings BASE

Beginning balance	688	
Net income	234	
Dividends (plug)	14	(688 + 234 – 908)
Ending balance	908	

OWC calculation

Inventories	98	108
Receivables	188	156
Prepaid items	45	54
Payables	(119)	(134)
Taxes payable	(88)	(96)
OWC	**124**	**88**

	Cash Flow Statement
Net income	234
Depreciation	275
Change in OWC	36
Operating cash flow	**545**
Capital expenditure	(364)
Investing cash flow	**(364)**
Change in debt	(196)
Change in common stock	10
Dividends	(14)
Financing cash flow	**(200)**
Net cash flow	**(19)**
Beginning cash	**1,019**
Ending cash	**1,000**

OTHER CASH FLOW PRESENTATIONS:

Most countries report their cash flows categorized into operating,
investing and financing flows. The most notable exception is the UK
which has many more sub-divisions in their presentation structure.

Ratio Analysis

There are four main areas that we must consider when covering ratio analysis. These are:

- Liquidity and solvency ratios
- Efficiency ratios
- Profitability
- Return ratios.

SOME POINTS TO NOTE ABOUT RATIO ANALYSIS:

There are often many variations about the detail of calculating a particular ratio and as you become experienced, you too will have views about the best way to do this. At this stage it is important to note that it is always vital to compare like with like and that more valuable information will be gleaned by trend analysis and benchmarking than by any metric in isolation.

You must always be very careful about generalizations about "what is good" and "what is bad". This is often very sector specific and what may be outrageous for one industry may be within the acceptable norm for another.

LIQUIDITY AND SOLVENCY

LONG - TERM:

Businesses can source funding from lenders or shareholders. Lenders have more security because interest *must* be paid and they rank before shareholders in the event of the business being wound up. Lenders sometimes increase their levels of security by legally "ringfencing" some of the business assets. In the event of default they can then force the liquidation of these assets, with the proceeds being used to repay the loan. Because their level of risk is lower than that of shareholders, the cost of debt finance is correspondingly lower. Interest is also tax deductible (in most countries) whereas dividends are not. This means that the after tax cost of debt is less than the equivalent cost of equity. As a result of this, a certain level of debt is desirable. *The big question is: how much?* The problem is that with too much debt there is a high risk of default and winding up. This is because the interest and capital payments relating to debt *must* be paid on their due dates, whereas dividend payments are *optional.*

There are two common metrics that are used to measure the relative level of debt and equity funding.

- The first is the proportion of debt relative to equity and is called *leverage or gearing.*
- The second measures the affordability of that debt and is called *interest cover.*

LIQUIDITY RATIOS LONG-TERM

Leverage or gearing ratio:

prudent level = less than 50%

$$\frac{Debt}{Debt + Equity}$$

Interest cover or times interest earned:

$$\frac{EBIT}{Interest\ expense}$$

© Adkins Matchett & Toy 2007   4   **AdkinsMatchett&Toy**

Some people calculate leverage by comparing debt/equity, so you should always ensure that you are comparing like with like.

Businesses that can withstand high leverage generally have two characteristics:

- A strong asset base to act as security; and
- Stable positive cash flows

For example, a young technology company should not have a high leverage ratio whereas a hotel chain business could very well carry lots of debt relative to equity.

The interest cover metric tells you how many times the profit before interest is greater than the interest expense. For example, if interest is covered 4 times, then operating profit would need to fall by a factor of 4 before the interest cost was not met. You can then form a view about how likely such a drop is.

Peel Inc – Leverage and interest cover!

The following are extracts from the balance sheet and income statement of Peel Inc. Calculate leverage (debt / debt + equity) and interest cover for last year and this year.

	Last year	This year
Inventories	850	932
Receivables	960	1,035
Prepaid items	488	494
Marketable securities	628	688
Cash	1,066	1,444
Accounts payable	803	892
Taxes payable	98	108
Dividends payable	188	156
Short-term debt	45	54
Current portion of long-term debt	1,019	1,000
Long-term debt	2,153	2,210
Provisions	654	678
Common stock	1,119	1,134
Additional paid in capital	1,188	1,196
Retained earnings	1,100	1,904
Operating profit	988	1,236
Interest expense	190	206

	Last Year	This Year
Debt	$3,217	$3,264

Last year (45 + 1,019 + 2,153)

This year (54 + 1,000 + 2,210)

Equity	$3,407	$4,234

Last year (1,119 + 1,188 + 1,100)

This year (1,134 + 1,196 + 1,904)

Leverage	48.57%	43.53%

Last year 3,217 / (3,217 + 3,407)

This year 3,264 / (3,264 + 4,234)

Interest cover	5.2 x	6.0 x

Last year (988 / 190)

This year (1,236 / 206)

Sometimes, you will see debt described as net debt. This means that any cash balances have been deducted from the debt. The debt used above ignores any cash balances and it sometimes referred to as gross debt. Either debt or net debt can be used to calculate leverage/gearing. This is a classic example of the variations in the detail of the calculation of these metrics and you must always be aware of what it is you are being presented with.

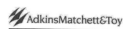

SHORT - TERM:

In the short-term, whether or not you can make that interest payment today is crucial. Many a profitable business has met its "holy grail" by having a short-term liquidity or solvency crisis. In some industries, this is the toughest part of the business.

There are two metrics that are commonly used to examine this area. They are the *current ratio* and the *quick ratio* (also called the *acid test*).

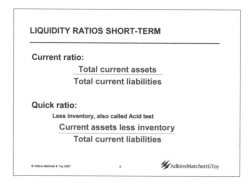

The current ratio examines how many times the short-term assets are greater than the short-term liabilities. The logic here is current assets (by definition) can be liquidated relatively quickly and that if some of the short-term liabilities need to be discharged then the current assets will always be available to do this. Of course, this is subject to the quality of the current assets.

However, inventories are often a significant component of current assets and in some sectors they are not necessarily easy to liquidate in the short-term, so the quick ratio or acid test applies the same logic but removes inventory from the equation. This therefore shows a more conservative view of the situation.

Peel Inc – Current and quick ratios.

Using the information above, calculate the current and quick ration for this year and last year.

	Last Year	This Year
Current assets	$3,992	$4,593
(850 + 960 + 488 + 628 + 1,066)		
(932 + 1,035 + 494 + 688 + 1,444)		
Current assets less inventory	$3,142	$3,661
(3,992 – 850)		
(4,593 – 932)		
Current liabilities	$2,153	$2,210
(803 + 98 + 188 + 45 + 1,019)		
(892 + 108 + 156 + 54 + 1,000)		
Current ratio	1.85 x	2.08 x
(3,992 / 2,153)		
(4,593 / 2,210)		
Quick ratio	1.46 x	1.66 x
(3,142 / 2,153)		
(3,661 / 2,210)		

EFFICIENCY RATIOS

There are a number of ratios that are commonly used to help form a view about the efficiency (or lack of it) of the assets of the business. There are several such ratios: days or turnover ratios are most often used for some working capital items but "% of" ratios are also used frequently. Let's examine each in turn:

DAYS OR TURNOVER RATIOS:

These ratios are commonly used for inventories, receivables and payables. They are usually calculated as follows:

OPERATING RATIOS

$$\text{Receivable days} = \frac{\text{Average receivables}}{\text{Sales}} \times 365$$

$$\text{Payable days} = \frac{\text{Average payables}}{\text{Cost of goods sold}} \times 365$$

$$\text{Inventory days} = \frac{\text{Average inventories}}{\text{Cost of goods sold}} \times 365$$

28

AdkinsMatchett&Toy

An average will usually be used for the working capital items but you will sometimes see these metrics calculated using the beginning or ending numbers only.

These ratios were explained in the chapter on working capital. You should review the relevant section if need be.

Some users prefer to "turn these ratios upside down" and look at "turnover" instead of days. Let's use inventories to examine this:

The days metric tells us the number of days, on average, that inventory sits in the warehouse before it is sold. It is calculated by finding out the % of COGS in the warehouse (inventory / COGS) and then applying this to the number of days in the year (365) to convert it into days.

INVENTORY / COGS * 365

Generally, the smaller this metric is the more efficient the business.

Inventory turn or turnover is calculated as follows:

COGS / INVENTORY

This tells us how many times the warehouse of inventory has been sold in the period. Generally, the bigger this metric the more efficient the business is. It does vary from industry to industry significantly. For example, you would expect a dairy to sell its inventories far quicker than, say, an airplane manufacturer.

Peel Inc – Days and turnover ratios!

COGS for Peel Inc for the year were $8,504. Calculate inventory days and inventory turn, using average inventories.

Average inventory   891
(850 + 932)/2
Inventory days   38
(891/8,504) * 365
Inventory turn   9.5 x
(8,504/891)

% OF RATIOS:
These ratios are normally calculated by reference to sales as follows:

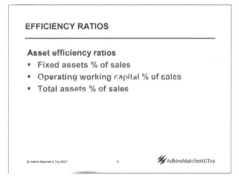

The size of a business will be a key Influencer in the amount of working capital needed. Therefore, it is useful to see what the relationship is.

Peel Inc – " % of " ratios!

For Peel, the sales numbers for last year and this year were $10,608 and $13,288 respectively. This means that operating working capital % of sales is as follows (using ending OWC):

	Last year	This year
OWC	1,397	1,461
(850 + 960 + 488 – 803 – 98)		
(932 + 1,035 + 494 – 892 – 108)		
OWC % Sales	13.17%	10.99%
(1,397 / 10,608)		
(1,461 / 13,288)		

This also tells us that Peel is more efficient this year compared with last year, since this year the OWC requirement is only 10.99% of sales compared with 13.17% last year.

If you are not familiar with the OWC calculation you should review the relevant section in the chapter on working capital.

PP&E OR FIXED ASSETS RATIOS:

% of ratios are also useful for fixed assets. These were discussed in the fixed assets chapter, which you should review if necessary. The ratios concerned are as follows:

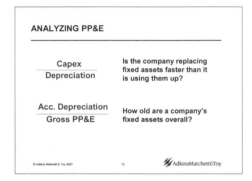

PROFITABILITY RATIOS

Margin calculations are the most commonly used measure of profitability. However, since there are many levels of profit given in an income statement, there are also many different margin calculations. The most common are as follows:

PROFITABILITY

Margins:

Gross margin %	=	$\dfrac{\text{Gross profit}}{\text{Sales}}$
Operating margin %	=	$\dfrac{\text{Operating profit}}{\text{Sales}}$
Net margin %	=	$\dfrac{\text{Net income}}{\text{Sales}}$
EBITDA margin %	=	$\dfrac{\text{EBITDA}}{\text{Sales}}$

© Adkins Matchett & Toy 2007   12   AdkinsMatchett&Toy

Peel Inc – margin calculations!

Peel's income statement for two years is as follows:

	Last year $	This year $
Sales	10,608	13,288
COGS	6,895	8,504
Gross profit	3,713	4,784
SG&A	2,725	3,548
Operating profit	988	1,236
Interest expense	190	206
Profit before tax	798	1,030
Tax expense	255	340
Net income	543	690

You are told that depreciation for both years was $730 and $790 respectively and amortization expense was $300 in both years.

Gross margin	35%	36%

Last year (3,713 / 10,608)

This year (4,784 / 13,288)

Operating profit margin	9.3%	9.3%

Last year (988 / 10,608)

This year (1,236 / 13,288)

Net income margin	5.1%	5.2%

Last year (543 / 10,608)

This year (690 / 13,288)

EBITDA	$2,018	$2,326

(988 + 730 + 300)

(1,236 + 790 + 300)

EBITDA margin	19.0%	17.5%

(2,018 / 10,608)

(2,326 / 13,288)

This business has gross margins of 35% and 36% but an operating profit margin that is significantly lower. This may be because they have an unreasonably high level of support cost, which may lead one to conclude that the business is inefficient. Alternatively, this level of support cost may be necessary because of the structure of the

business. This is particularly the case with businesses that make and sell branded goods. In fact, with these businesses the contrast between gross and operating margin can be even more extreme and it is driven by their very high level of marketing spend.

RETURN RATIOS

Return ratios seek to link the profit being earned with the investment required to earn it. You may have two opportunities of returning a profit of $10,000 but one requires an investment of $100,000 whereas the other requires $1,000,000. In profit terms they are both performing at the same level but in return terms the first is delivering a 10% return and the second delivering only 1%.

The main issue with calculating return in the context of a business is deciding what your view is of the "investment". Once you have made this decision, the next step is to select the "matching" level of profitability. There are many variations of how return ratios are calculated. Here we are going to concentrate on understanding the principle behind them.

For example, you may consider the investment to be shareholders' equity. Therefore, the level of profit should be net income since this is the profit available to pay to the shareholders.

Alternatively, you may want to include the capital provided by lenders in your calculation so that you are considering both equity and debt. In this case you need to take the profit before interest. This level of profit in the income statement is before taxes. Many practitioners will calculate an estimate of the tax on profit before interest, to give them a profit before interest but after taxes number.

Further possibility for variation arises when calculating these metrics depending upon whether you include the beginning, ending or average "investment" numbers.

Here are some examples of return ratios:

RETURN RATIOS

Return on assets % = $\dfrac{\text{Net income}}{\text{Average assets}}$

Return on equity % = $\dfrac{\text{Net income}}{\text{Average equity}}$

Return on invested capital % = $\dfrac{\text{Operating profit after tax}}{\text{Net PP\&E and OWC}}$

Peel Inc – return calculations!

Let's calculate the return for Peel, using shareholders' equity as our definition of investment. This is normally called return on equity (ROE) or return on shareholders' equity (ROSE). In the following example, we are going to use ending equity but many people use average instead.

Note: In the examples that follow, we are calculating ROE using the book numbers. You could also calculate this return using the market value of the equity. This is on the grounds that the opportunity cost for the shareholder is how much they are foregoing by not selling their shares at this price.

	Last Year	This Year
Shareholders' equity	$3,407	$4,234
Net income	$543	$690
Sales	$10,608	$13,288
ROE	15.94%	16.3%

Last year (543 / 3,407)
This year (690 / 4,234)

Net income margin	5.12%	5.19%

Last year (543 / 10,608)
This year (690 / 13,288)

Investment efficiency	3.11 x	3.14 x

(10,608 / 3,407)
(13,288 / 4,234)

So how can we put these together to tell the story? Last year, the return on shareholders' equity was 15.94%. This was delivered by making a margin of 5.12% on every dollar sold. For every dollar of investment, 3.11 dollars of sales were made. So the margin of 5.12% was made 3.11 times in the year leading to a return of 15.94% (5.12% * 3.11). This is called the **Dupont Formula** and it is very useful for making sense of the numbers.

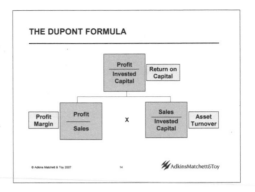

AND FINALLY!

Do not confine yourself to financial ratios. Some of the most telling indicators of performance use a mix of both financial and non-financial information. One of the most well known of these is used in the retail industry and is *sales per square foot*. (Or square meters depending upon which part of the world you live in!). Most of these are very industry specific and are very valuable and insightful.